Micro Ran

G000229402

- {

Short Walks
by the
Suffolk Coast

15 Walks on Suffolk's Coast and Tidal Rivers

Geoff and Yvonne Gostling

ISBN 0-9525478-8-0

Printed by Portman Press
Published by G J Gostling
Copyright © G J Gostling

To the best of my knowledge, information supplied in this book
is accurate, and rights of way were correct at the time of writing.
No responsibility is accepted for acts of trespass, problems arising
from rerouting of paths, or misread instructions.

CONTENTS

Foreword

Most of the walks in this book are extracted from other books in the Micro Rambler series. As in the other books, instructions for each individual walk are contained on the right-hand page, with the relevant map on the left, so there's no need to turn over pages while you're walking..

The average length of walks in this book is 5km (3 miles). The map scale for the walk maps is 4cm to 1km or 2½in to 1 mile.

All walks use 'Rights of Way', permissive paths or unclassified roads. Limited use is made of other roads for joining paths, or getting to and from car parks.

Distances are given in metres and kilometres. If you're more at home with yards and miles, it may be of help to remember that 1 yard is about 1 metre, 800 metres is a half-mile, 1½km is about 1 mile.

Times are based on average walking speeds. As a rough guide, at an average walking speed, it takes about 12 minutes to walk 1km, or just over 1 minute to walk 100m.

Country Walking

Right of Way means that you have a right of passage over the ground, but no right to stray from the path. You also have a right to expect that paths be unobstructed. Clearly farmers have to work the land, but footpaths should be rolled within 2 weeks of ploughing, if weather permits.

Please remember the Country Code. Machinery, livestock and crops are the farmers livelihood. Help them, and help preserve wildlife by observing a few simple rules:

Guard against risk of fire;	Take litter home
Protect wildlife plants & trees;	Use gates & stiles to cross fences;
Fasten gates;	Leave livestock alone;
Keep pets under control;	Don't pollute water;
Keep to rights of way;	Don't make unnecessary noise;

Introduction

Most of the walks in this book are taken from books in the 'Micro Rambler' series. As the name suggests, all walks involve at least some walking on the coast or by tidal rivers. Normally they should present no problem, but at some high tides they could be covered. If so, take an alternative route if available, or wait for the tide to drop.

All walks are contained in Landranger Sheets 156 and 169, and you may find these useful in getting to start points. (Grid references are provided in the heading information for each walk). The outline map inside the front cover should also help.

About the Area (For related walks, see index on page 36)

Alde (River)   A 10 mile shingle bank stretching from Aldeburgh to Shinglestreet, results in 3 rivers sharing the same river mouth (Ore, Alde and Butley) Constant changes of direction were a nightmare for barges, as they sailed to Snape Maltings.

Aldeburgh A seaside town, full of character. Benjamin Britten and Peter Pears are buried in the churchyard of St Peter and Paul, along with other eminent musicians. There are many interesting buildings, the most famous of which is the Moot Hall.

Blyth (River)   The tidal expanse of Bulcamp marshes drains so fast through the narrow channel at Walberswick that small boats often need help getting into Southwold Harbour. Long ago the river mouth was further south, and formed the ancient port of Dunwich.

Blythburgh   Few people travelling the A12 can fail to admire the church of Holy Trinity, standing high above surrounding marshes.   There are other interesting buildings in the village too - well worth a look round after your walk.

Boyton   There's an attractive group of almshouses next to the church. The church has a well preserved Norman doorway in the north wall. One pub, the Bell.

Butley (River). Once called Butley Creek, and even now the Ferry is called Butley Creek Ferry. You can cross on this and walk to Orford, (but it's a 5 mile round trip)

Deben (River)   Thought by many to be one of the most attractive rivers in East Anglia, not only for sailing, but also for walkers.   There's a network of paths on both sides, and the sandy soil makes for excellent walking at all times of the year.

Dunwich   In King John's day, this was only slightly smaller than Ipswich, with 9 churches and 2 monasteries. Most of it now lies under the sea, and not one of the original churches remains. Now there are a few houses, The Ship pub, a prize winning museum, a good fish and chip restaurant, and the gateway to Greyfriars priory.

Eastbridge A quaint village near Minsmere Nature Reserve. There's an excellent pub, The Eel's Foot. The village must have been popular with smugglers.

Harkstead A pleasant village, with a nice 14th century church. There's a good pub, The Baker's Arms.

Holbrook is best known for the Royal Hospital School, once a boarding school for the sons of naval officers. It's now co-ed. Church has connections with Anne Boleyn.

Iken St Botolph's church stands on a promontory above the Alde. It may have been built on the site of St. Botolph's Abbey, a place of pilgrimage. The church still is.

Ore (River) The River Ore is only known by that name as far as slightly north of Orford, when it becomes the River Alde - see above.

Orford An attractive village, with much too see, including Orford Castle, and a church with a ruined Norman chancel. There are several places of refreshment.

Orwell (River). Probably the only Suffolk river still used by commercial traffic. There's more or less continuous walking along the shore from the Royal Harwich Yacht Club at Woolverstone to Shotley Point. Shares an estuary with the *Stour*.

Pin Mill The name comes from a mill on the River Pindle. One of the most pictured pubs in Suffolk, the Butt and Oyster, stands on the edge of the river Orwell.

Ramsholt It once had 240 parishioners, but there are few now. There is a small church with a round or oval tower, and a popular riverside pub, the Ramsholt Arms.

Snape There are lots of things to see in the Snape concert hall complex, including antiques, arts and crafts, clothing shops, a good pub and a café. As for the rest of the village - if it hadn't been for grave robbers, the Saxon ship found on Church Common might have made Snape as well known archaeologically as Sutton Hoo.

Southwold You could almost be stepping back in time, due to the haphazard grouping of buildings, interspersed by greens. A fire in 1659 destroyed most of the town, and as a result spaces were left as firebreaks during the rebuilding. The town is also a popular seaside resort, and very crowded in the summer.

Stour (River). This is the widest river of any on the Suffolk coast, and forms the border between Suffolk and Essex. It shares an estuary with the *Orwell*.

Thorpeness became popular when the Meare was excavated in 1910. The House in the Clouds was once a water tower. There's also a postmill. One pub, The Dolphin.

Walberswick This attractive and popular village is probably best visited on a weekday in the summer months.   There are various places of refreshment.

Waldringfield   A popular village with sailors and walkers. The Maybush, on the riverside, serves good food and beer.

Map 1

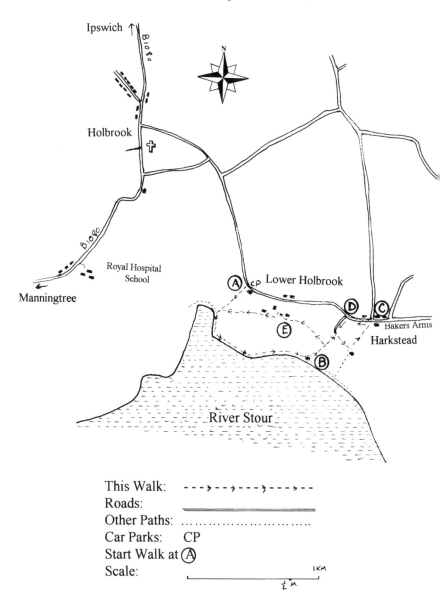

This Walk: - - -＞- -＞- - -＞- - -＞- -
Roads: ════════════
Other Paths: ....
Car Parks: CP
Start Walk at Ⓐ
Scale:

Walk 1

Distance: 4½km, (3m) 1-1½ hours
Start Point: Lower Holbrook (GR 177351)
Route: Lower Holbrook, Harkstead
Pubs: Bakers Arms, Harkstead
Going: Easy, but can be slippery when wet
Car Park: Small Free Car Park in Lower Holbrook

How to get there   *From Holbrook, on the B1080 between Ipswich and Manningtree, take the road signposted Harkstead. The car park is in Lower Holbrook, on the right, just after a left hand bend and difficult to spot coming from the Harkstead direction.*

A: Leave the car park and go down the track towards the river. In about 300m you'll reach the head of Holbrook Creek. Here keep straight on along the left hand side of the creek to reach the river bank. After about 1km on the river bank you'll reach a cottage.

B: Follow the field-edge path round to the left to pass the cottage and immediately turn left up a clear track to reach a narrow lane. Turn right on the lane for about 150m, then turn left uphill on a grassy path. This brings you out on a side road next to the **Bakers Arms.**

C: When you reach the main road next to the Bakers Arms, turn left to follow the road slightly downhill for about 250m to reach a narrow lane on the left.

D: Turn left on the narrow lane, and after rounding the bend in about 100m turn right, briefly retracing your steps towards the riverside cottage. In about 100m, before reaching the cottage, take the path across the field to the right signed 'Footpath to Holbrook Creek'.

E: In about 500m, follow waymarks taking you across a driveway, and through some trees. Keep left to reach a footpath sign, where you can turn left taking you back onto the field edge path again. Continue along for about another 500m to return to the track by Holbrook Creek. Here turn right to return to the car park.

Map 2

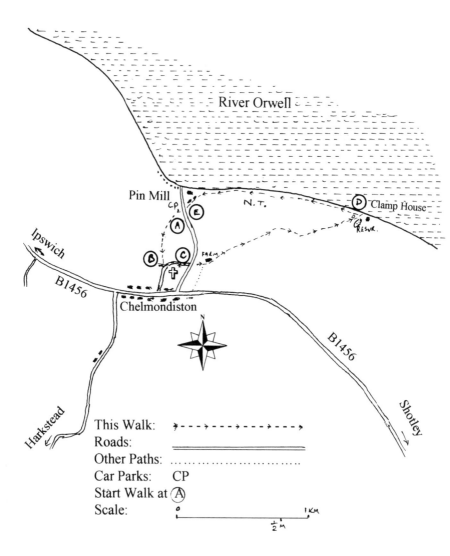

River Orwell

Pin Mill

CP

E

A

N.T.

Clamp House

RESVR.

Ipswich

B

C

FARM

B1456

Chelmondiston

N

B1456

Harkstead

Shotley

This Walk: ＋- - - ＋- - - ＋- - - ＋- - - ＋

Roads: ════════════════

Other Paths: ....

Car Parks: CP

Start Walk at Ⓐ

Scale:
0   1 KM

½ M

Walk 2

Distance: 4km, (2½m) 1 hour approx
Start Point: Pin Mill (GR 206378)
Route: Pin Mill, Clamp House, N.T. Woods
Pub: Butt and Oyster, Pin Mill
Going: Easy, but the track down to the river is muddy after rain
Car Park: Pay and Display Car Park in Pin Mill

How to get there: *Take the B1456 from Ipswich to Shotley. In Chelmondiston, take the signposted left turn to Pin Mill. The car park is near the bottom on the left.*

A: Go through the picnic site next to the car park, and cross the stile at the far end. Turn right and then immediately left over another stile to enter a large 'L-shaped' sloping field. Go diagonally uphill to reach a metal gate and stile at the top. Cross the stile and continue along the unsurfaced lane.

B: When you reach the top of the lane, turn left, and take the narrow road to the left of the church. Stay on the narrow road to reach a T-junction.

C: At the T-junction, go straight across on the signed bridleway. In about 100m the path joins a surfaced farm road. Keep straight on along the road, which becomes a cart track after the farm buildings. Stay on the track for about 1½km to reach a gate into a lane bearing the sign 'Clamp House - Footpath only'. Continue down this lane towards the river.

D: Just after passing a reedy pond on the left, turn left between the pond and a small pantiled barn, to reach a clear path through the National Trust woods. Stay on the main path, more or less parallel to the river, eventually following it round behind some houses in Pin Mill.

E. After passing behind the houses the path swings right taking you down to a road. Keep straight ahead down a flight of steps to reach the road near the car park, a few steps to the right The **Butt and Oyster** is on the riverside further down the road.

Map 3

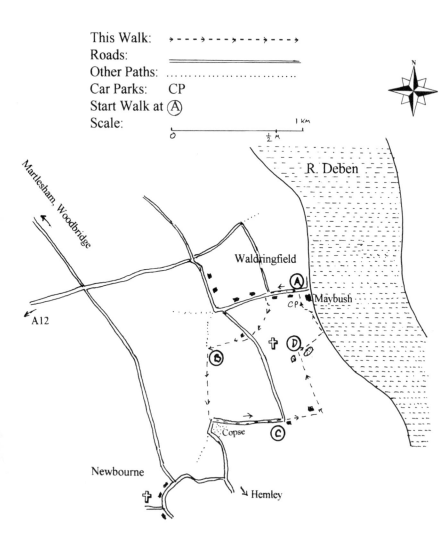

This Walk: + - - - + - - - + - - - + - - - +
Roads:
Other Paths: ....
Car Parks: CP
Start Walk at Ⓐ
Scale:

1 Km

0   ½ M

R. Deben

Martlesham, Woodbridge

Waldringfield

Ⓐ

Maybush

CP

A12

✝

Ⓓ

Ⓑ

Copse

Ⓒ

Newbourne

✝

Hemley

Walk 3

Distance: 4km, (2½m) 1 hour approximately
Start Point: Waldringfield (GR285445)
Route: Waldringfield circular
Pubs: Maybush
Going: Easy but muddy and slippery in places after rain
Car Park: Public car park behind Maybush car park.

__How to get there:__   *Waldringfield is signposted from the A12, between the A14 and Woodbridge. Follow the road through the village as far as the Maybush.*

A: Go down to the road by the Maybush and turn left up the road away from the river. In about 300m, just after passing the second lane on the right, turn left on a signed track. In about 75m go through the gap into the field on the right and take the path across the field towards a cream coloured cottage. Go down the path to the left of the cottage.

B: In 350m turn left in a shady lane, soon continuing through open fields. When you reach the road by a small copse, turn left on the road towards the river.

C: In about 600m, where the road bends left back towards Waldringfield, go straight on down a pleasant lane, immediately passing a cottage. In 300m, (about 50m after passing a house on the left), turn left on the signed path, soon across open fields.

D: In about 500m you'll pass between 2 large ponds. Immediately after this, turn right towards the river. When you reach the shore, turn left on the signed path to return to Waldringfield. The flight of steps in about 250m will take you back to the car parks, or continue along the shore to reach the Maybush, if the tide permits.

Map 4

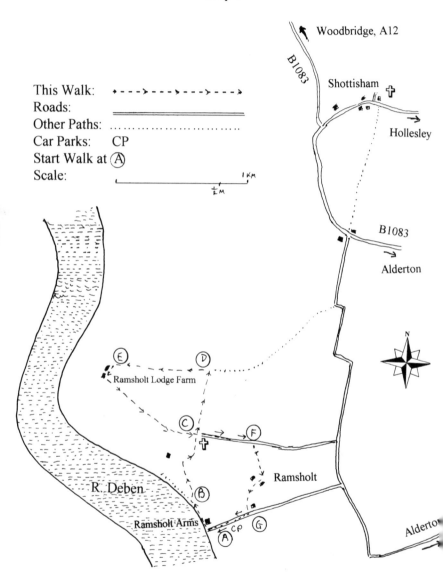

Woodbridge, A12

B1083

Shottisham

Hollesley

This Walk: → - - - → - - - → - - - → - - - →
Roads: ══════════
Other Paths: ·················
Car Parks: CP
Start Walk at Ⓐ
Scale: |————————————| 1 KM
              |½ M

B1083

Alderton

N

Ⓔ → → → Ⓓ
Ramsholt Lodge Farm

Ⓒ
✝
Ⓕ

R. Deben

Ramsholt

Ⓑ

Ramsholt Arms

Ⓐ CP Ⓖ

Alderto

Walk 4

Distance: 4½km (3m) 1 hour approx
Start Point: Ramsholt (GR 309414)
Route: Figure-eight walk round Ramsholt church, and Ramsholt
Pubs: Ramsholt Arms
Going: Easy
Parking: Free grass public car park in Ramsholt

How to get there: *Take the B1083 from Woodbridge. At the T-junction at Shottisham, turn right, still on the B1083. Take the first right, and Ramsholt is the second turning on the right.*

A: Go out of the bottom corner (nearest the road) of the car park, and walk down towards the river. Turn right along the footpath between the pub and the river, and in about 100m turn right to pass through a gate into a water meadow.

B: Follow the path across the meadow. This bends to the right, eventually bringing you into a sunken lane, leading up to the left hand side of the church.

C: Go straight across the sand-blown road next to the church and onto the field edge track on the other side.

D: In about 500m at a T-junction, turn left, and keep straight on for about 800m. *On a clear day, you'll be able to see all the way up the River Deben as far as Martlesham creek on this stretch.*

E: At the T-junction, turn left to pass a cottage and farm buildings. In about 150m turn left again and you'll be heading back towards the church. Continue along this sandy road, passing the church again in about 800m.

F: About 500m after the church, turn right on a clear signed track. In about 300m it bends right, passing the old school house. After this, by a thatched cottage, follow the grassy track round to the left, soon heading uphill in a lane.. This brings you out on the Ramsholt road in about 300m.

G: Turn right on the road to return to the car park in about 200m.

Map 5

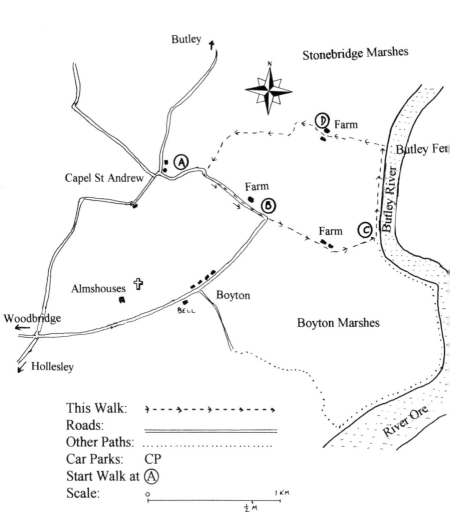

Butley

Stonebridge Marshes

Ⓓ Farm

Butley Fer...

Capel St Andrew

Ⓐ

Farm

Ⓑ

Farm

Butley River

Ⓒ

Almshouses ✝

Boyton

BELL

Boyton Marshes

Woodbridge
←

Hollesley

River Ore

This Walk: ＞- - -＞- - -＞- - -＞- - -＞
Roads: ══════════════
Other Paths: ....
Car Parks: CP
Start Walk at Ⓐ
Scale: o   1 KM
                        ½ M

- 14 -

Walk 5

Distance:	4km (2½m) 1 hour approximately
Start Point:	Capel St Andrew (GR 378480)
Route:	Boyton, Boyton Marshes, Butley Ferry
Pubs:	None on route , but try the Oyster Inn at Butley.
Going:	Fairly Easy
Car Parking:	Roadside verge parking only.

How to get there: *Take the B1083 from Woodbridge. Turn left on the Hollesley road past the old Woodbridge Airfield. At Hollesley, turn left towards Butley. Take the <u>second</u> signposted right turn to Boyton, by some conspicuous red brick farm buildings. Follow the road round to the left, then park on one of the wide verges near the sharp right-hand bend in about 300m.*

A: After leaving the car, continue on the road, passing the lane leading to Butley Ferry.   Stay on the road for about another 500m as far as the sharp right hand bend towards Boyton village.

B: At the right hand bend take the signposted farm road straight ahead. Shortly after passing farm buildings in about 400m follow the slightly raised track across Boyton marshes to reach the Butley river wall

C: Turn left on the river wall.   In about 800m, when you reach the jetty serving Butley Ferry, leave the river bank via a stile and follow the clear track to pass between farm buildings in about 400m.

D: Stay on the concrete farm road all the way back through Stonebridge marshes to reach your start point.

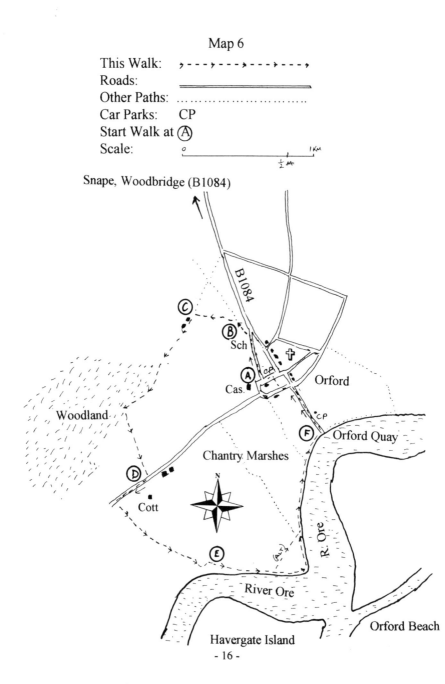

Map 6

This Walk: ╺ - - ╺ - - ╺ - - ╺ - - ╺
Roads: ══════════
Other Paths: ....
Car Parks: CP
Start Walk at Ⓐ
Scale: 0 ———————— 1 KM
½ Mⁱˡ

Snape, Woodbridge (B1084)

B1084

Ⓒ

Ⓑ
Sch

Ⓐ
Cas.

Orford

Woodland

CP

Ⓕ
Orford Quay

Chantry Marshes

N

Ⓓ

Cott

R. Ore

Ⓔ

(A..)

River Ore

Orford Beach

Havergate Island

- 16 -

Walk 6

Distance:	7km (4½m) 1½-2 hours
Start Point:	Market Hill, Orford (GR 421499)
Route:	Orford Circular
Pubs:	Kings Head, Jolly Sailor, Crown and Castle Hotel
Going:	Fairly easy
Car Parking:	Market Hill, or the large car park opposite the Jolly Sailor down towards the quay (in this case, start at **F**).

A: Leave Market Hill by the road almost opposite the Crown and Castle Hotel. Pass the park on the left, then, just before the main road, turn left along an unmade road in front of the school.

B: Soon after passing the school, turn left on a signposted path diagonally across the field, heading about 50m to the right of two bungalows.

C: When you reach the other side of the field, turn left to pass the bungalows. In about 500m, at the corner of a wood, stay on the main track following the edge of the wood. In another 350m it swings left away from the wood bringing you down to a narrow road in about 400m.

D: Turn right on the road, then about 200m after passing a cottage set well back from the road, turn left down a signed track towards the river. Stay on this to reach the river bank in about 800m.

E: Follow the sign taking you up the river bank to the left, and stay on the bank all the way back to Orford Quay. (If you are feeling tired, save yourself a few steps by taking the short cut shown on the map opposite!)

F: Go straight up the road from the quay for about 400m, to reach a crossroads. Turn left at the cross roads, and in about 100m turn right along Bakers Lane. After passing the smoke house on the left you'll reach Market Hill.

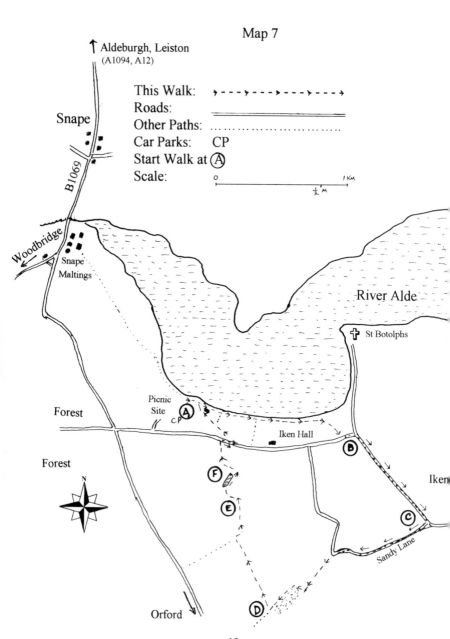

Map 7

This Walk: ▸- - -▸- - -▸- - -▸- - - ▸
Roads: _____
Other Paths: ....
Car Parks: CP
Start Walk at Ⓐ
Scale: 0 _____ 1 Km
               ½ M

↑ Aldeburgh, Leiston
(A1094, A12)

Snape

B1069

Woodbridge

Snape
Maltings

River Alde

✝ St Botolphs

Forest

Picnic
Site
CP
Ⓐ

Iken Hall

Ⓑ

Forest

Ⓕ

Ⓔ

Iken

Ⓒ

N

Sandy Lane

Orford

Ⓓ

Walk 7

Distance:	5½km (3½m) 1-1½ hours (7km inc St Botolph's church)
Start Point:	Picnic Site, Iken (GR 400563)
Route:	Iken Cliff, and St Botolph's church, (Optional)
Pub:	Not on route but for refreshments, try Snape Maltings
Going:	Easy, but the tide can cover the beach in 'A'
Car Parking:	As above

How to get there: *From Snape, take the Orford road. Turn left at the crossroads, signposted Iken, and then take the next left for the picnic site*

A: Leave the picnic site by the path in the bottom right hand corner. Where the paths cross, take the one towards the shore. Ignore the first two signed paths leaving the shore and continue until the path gradually leaves the shore, over some wooden steps, to emerge on a narrow road.

B: Turn left on the road. (*St. Botolph's church is 700m down the lane on the left when you reach the bend). C*ontinue on the road round the right hand bend. Stay on this road for about 900m as far as Sandy Lane.

C: Turn right into Sandy Lane. In 800m, where the road bends sharp right, continue on a sandy track more or less straight ahead. Follow the track along a thin line of silver birch for about 300m, then turn right by a small wood. Stay on the track alongside the wood when it bends left, to reach a gateway in about 200m.

D: After passing through the gateway, turn right on a wide track with a tree belt on your right hand side. When you get to the T-junction at the end, turn briefly right then left on a wide track with a wood on your left.

E: In 250m, follow the edge of the wood as it bends to the left. The path goes gently downhill along the edge of the wood for about 200m, then bends sharp right along the edge of a deep reservoir hidden in trees. In about 250m you'll reach the head of the reservoir, where you should turn left on a metalled farm road.

F: Soon after joining the farm road cross a stile into a field on the right. Go uphill towards the top left hand corner, to reach a stile onto a narrow road. Turn right on the road for about 100m, then turn sharp left on a signed path. Keep more or less straight ahead on this path to return to the picnic site.

Map 8

This Walk: ❯ - - ❯ - - ❯ - - - ❯ - - - ❯ - -
Roads:
Other Paths: . . . .
Car Parks: CP
Start Walk at Ⓐ
Scale:

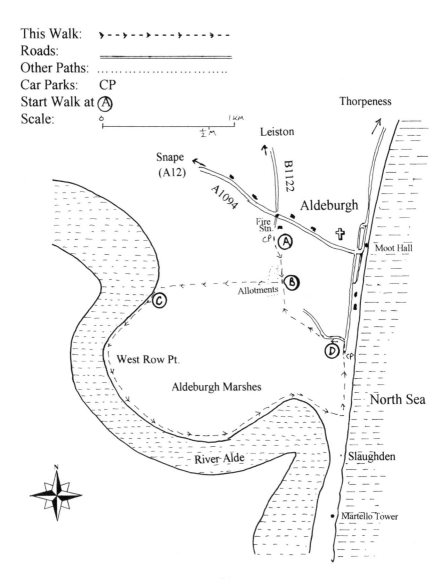

Walk 8

Distance: 6km (3½m) 1-1½ hours
Start Point: Kings Field, Aldeburgh (GR 458569)
Route: Aldeburgh Marshes, River Alde bank, West Row Point
Pub: Various in Aldeburgh
Going: Fairly Easy
Car Park: Kings Field car park (Access from Leiston Rd Roundabout signed 'Fire Station')

A: Go across the field towards the gap in the corner between the red-brick wall and the hedge surrounding the allotments.   In about 75m look for a signposted path on the right through the allotments.

B: Take the path through the allotments, and then keep more or less straight on via a series of bridges and gates. In about 500m go straight on across a sandy track, to reach the river wall in about another 400m.

C: Turn left on the river wall. You'll find that you're still walking away from Aldeburgh, but at West Row Point you'll start turning back towards the town again. Continue along the wall for about another 1½km to reach a car park by the beach. Turn left on the unmade road towards the town, and walk along as far as Park Road (the first road on the left) .

D: Turn left up Park Road. In about 300m, where the road becomes a private road, take the left fork, signposted Kings Field. Continue along on the main path, soon following a red brick wall, to bring you back to the recreation ground car park.

Map 9

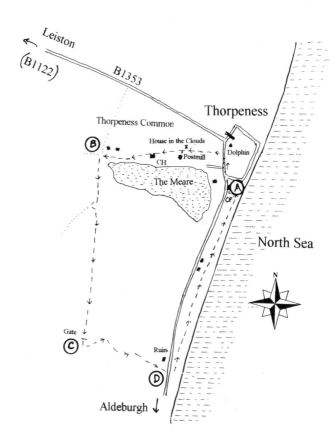

This Walk: » - - - » - - - » - - - » - - - »
Roads: ════════
Other Paths: ....
Car Parks: CP
Start Walk at Ⓐ
Scale:
0   1 KM
½ M

Walk 9

Distance:	5½km (3½m) 1½ hours approx
Start Point:	Thorpeness (GR 472596)
Route:	Thorpeness Common, Thorpeness beach
Pub:	The Dolphin, Thorpeness
Going:	Easy, but the path over the water meadows is very slippery when wet or during the winter months
Car Park:	Public car park near the beach

How to get there: *Approaching from Aldeburgh, take the beach road north. The car park is on the right, just before reaching the Meare. (Approaching from Aldringham, turn right when you reach the village).*

A: Turn right out of the car park, and walk along the main road past the Meare. After passing the Golf Club road, turn left on a footpath on an unmade road signed Thorpeness windmill. Keep more or less straight on to pass between the House in the Clouds and the windmill. Continue on past the Golf Club onto a signed path. In about another 600m, after passing alongside the Meare with the golf course on your right, you'll reach a group of cottages.

B: At the cross-track near the cottages, turn left on the old railway line, now a shady path. Stay on this for about 400m, soon passing the head of the Meare. Just after the path bends sharp right, go through a gateway on the left back onto the old railway, now a permissive footpath. Continue along this pleasant grassy track to reach a metal gate in about 1km.

C: Immediately after the gate turn left on a signed fenced footpath. Stay on this raised path across low-lying water meadows to emerge on the Thorpeness - Aldeburgh road, near a small ruined bungalow.

D: Cross the road and turn left on the shore to return to Thorpeness. When you reach the first of the houses, stay on the beach side. The car park is about 600m further on.

Map 10

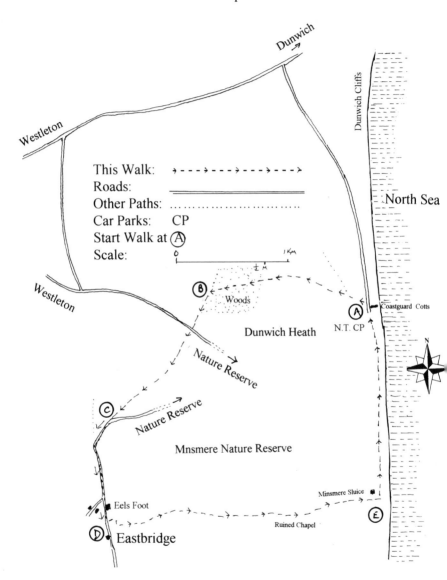

This Walk: →- - -→- - -→- - -→- - -→

Roads: ──────

Other Paths: ....

Car Parks: CP

Start Walk at Ⓐ

Scale: 0   1 KM

Dunwich

Westleton

Westleton

Dunwich Cliffs

North Sea

Ⓑ Woods

Dunwich Heath

Nature Reserve

Ⓐ Coastguard Cotts

N.T. CP

Ⓒ Nature Reserve

Mnsmere Nature Reserve

Minsmere Sluice

Eels Foot

Ruined Chapel

Ⓔ

Ⓓ Eastbridge

N

Walk 10

Distance:	8km (5 m) 1½-2½ hours
Start Point:	Coastguard Cottages, Dunwich (GR 477677)
Route:	North Walks, Eastbridge, Minsmere Beach
Pub:	The Eels Foot, Eastbridge
Going:	Fairly easy, but longer than average for this book
Car Parking:	N.T. Car Park - Free to members

How to get there: *Westleton and Dunwich are signposted from the A12 just north of Yoxford. From Westleton take the Dunwich road then take the second road on the right to reach the N.T. car park.*

A. From the car park, go back along the access road. Almost opposite the line of cottages, turn left on a signed path across the heath. Keep more or less straight on along the main path for about 700m, until it bends to the right along the edge of some woodland. Here go straight on into the wood. Follow this pleasant path for about 700m to reach a T-junction.

B: Turn left at the T-junction. In about 400m cross a road and continue on a grassy open path. In a further 600m the path enters woodland and descends to join the Minsmere nature reserve road.

C: Continue on the road in the same direction as before . In about 300m follow the road as it bends left. In another 600m you'll reach the **Eels Foot** pub on the left.

D: About 100m after the Eels Foot, turn left on a path signposted to Minsmere Sluice. In 50m follow signs taking you to the right, then after turning left again, follow the clear path for about 2½km all the way down to the red brick sluice.

E: When you reach the sluice, turn left, and follow the dune path along to the coastguard cottages in about 1½km.

Map 11

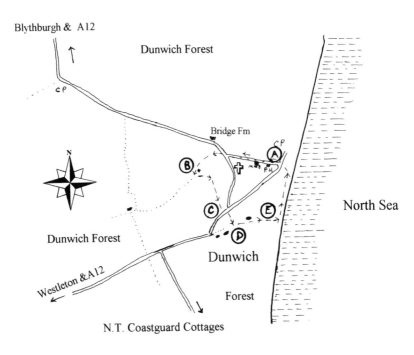

Blythburgh & A12

Dunwich Forest

CP

Bridge Fm

(A)

(B)

(C)

(E)

North Sea

N

Dunwich Forest

(D)

Dunwich

Westleton & A12

Forest

N.T. Coastguard Cottages

This Walk:	⟩ - - - ⟩ - - - ⟩ - - - ⟩ - - - ⟩
Roads:	═══════
Other Paths:	....
Car Parks:	CP
Start Walk at	(A)
Scale:	0 ——————— 1 KM
	½ M

Walk 11

Distance: 3km (2 m) 45m - 1hr
Start Point: Beach Car Park, Dunwich (GR 479708)
Route: Dunwich Circular
Pub: Ship Inn, Dunwich
Going: Easy, but please note that Dunwich Cliffs are still
eroding - take due care and stay away from the edge.
Car Parking: As above

How to get there: *Westleton and Dunwich are signposted from the A12 just north of Yoxford.*

A: Go back along the road, and walk up past the Ship Inn, the museum and the church. After passing the church, take the signed R.U.P.P. (Road used as Public Path) a few steps to the right of the War Memorial. Follow this for about 400m to pass Walnut Tree and Apple Tree cottages.

B: Shortly after passing the cottages, turn sharp left on a signed path. Follow the field edge uphill, and then round to the right when you reach the corner. In about 400m you'll reach a narrow road.

C: At the road turn left for about 75m, to reach a narrow path on the right. *(If you get as far as the road on the left, you've missed it!)* Follow this shady path to reach an unmade road in about 150m.

D: Turn left on the unmade road and stay on it to reach Dunwich Cliffs in about 400m. (Mind your head on the low bridge!).

E: Turn left on the clearly signed path along the top of the cliffs, soon passing along the back of the Friary ruins, to reach the road near the Ship Inn in Dunwich in about 500m.

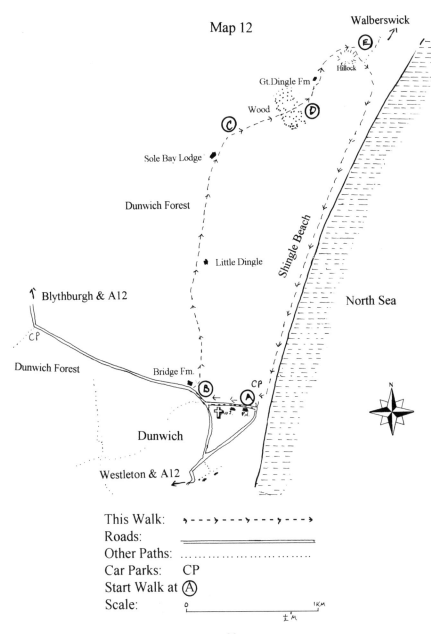

Map 12

Walberswick

E

Hillock

Gt.Dingle Fm

Wood

D

C

Sole Bay Lodge

Dunwich Forest

Little Dingle

Shingle Beach

↑ Blythburgh & A12

CP

North Sea

Dunwich Forest

Bridge Fm.

CP

B

A

Dunwich

Westleton & A12 ←

N

This Walk: ›‐‐‐›‐‐‐›‐‐‐›‐‐‐›
Roads: ══════════
Other Paths: ....
Car Parks: CP
Start Walk at Ⓐ
Scale: 0 _____ 1KM
½ M

- 28 -

Walk 12

Distance:	7½km (4½ m) 1½-2 hours
Start Point:	Beach Car Park, Dunwich (GR 479708)
Route:	Dunwich Forest, Dunwich Beach
Pub:	Ship Inn, Dunwich
Going:	Mostly easy, but hard work on the beach.
Car Parking:	As above

How to get there: *Westleton and Dunwich are signed from the A12 just north of Yoxford. When you reach Dunwich, follow the road as far as you can to reach the beach car park*

A: Walk along the road passing the Ship Inn and Dunwich Museum. Just after passing the church follow the road round to the right. Shortly after crossing the bridge you'll reach a signed bridleway to the right.

B: Turn right on the bridleway, keeping to the right of farm buildings. Stay on the main track for about 2km, following frequent signs for the 'Suffolk Coast and Heaths Path'. 300m after passing 'Sole Bay Lodge', a white weatherboarded bungalow, the track bends right, away from the edge of the forest and becomes a hedged lane.

C: Follow the hedged lane slightly downhill - you should get some good views of Westwood Marshes over to the left. At the bottom of the lane pass through the gate and continue through the small wood.

D: On the other side of the wood, follow the Suffolk Coast and Heaths Path signs round to the right of Great Dingle Hill. (12m high!) Follow the clear path round to the other side of the hill to reach a path on a low bank. Turn right on the path, which will take you to the left of a small hillock. The path then swings right towards the shore, and soon you'll reach a signed T-junction with a well used path.

E: Turn right on the path and follow it to reach the shore in about 400m. Turn right on the shore to reach Dunwich in about 2½km.

Map 13

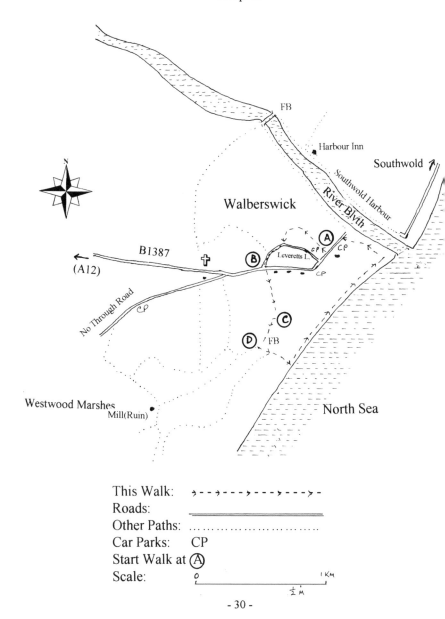

FB

Harbour Inn

Southwold

Southwold Harbour

River Blyth

Walberswick

B1387

(A12)

Ⓐ

CP

CP

Ⓑ

Leveretts L.

CP

No Through Road

CP

Ⓒ

Ⓓ

FB

Westwood Marshes

Mill(Ruin)

North Sea

This Walk: >- - ->- - ->- - ->- - ->-
Roads: ════════
Other Paths: ....
Car Parks: CP
Start Walk at Ⓐ
Scale: 0   1 Km
                                        ½ M

Walk 13

Distance:	3km (2 m) 1 hour approx
Start Point:	Beach Car Park, Walberswick (GR 500749)
Route:	Walberswick, Westwood Marshes, and the beach
Pub:	The Bell Inn
Going:	Fairly easy
Car Parking:	Soon after passing the village green, park in the long narrow car park on the left

How to get there: *Walberswick is signed from the A12 just south of Blythburgh.*

A: Go to the back of the long narrow car park at the end nearest the village. Go down the bank and cross the stile into the low lying meadow. Keep straight on to join a reedy ditch along the left hand side of the field, and follow it to reach a stile into a lane in about 200m. Cross the stile and turn left up the lane to reach the road (Leverett's Lane). Turn right in the road and follow it to reach the main road in about 300m.

B: When you reach the main road, go down the signed footpath opposite. Follow this clear path towards Westwood Marshes, keeping close to the field edge all the way down to the bottom of the field.

C: At the bottom follow the field edge round to the right for about 50m, to find a path through the bushes onto the marsh. Follow the boarded walkway through reeds for about 150m to the river bank.

D: Turn right on the river bank to the footbridge, and cross the river. Follow the clear path to reach the beach in about 300m. Turn left on the beach and walk along almost as far as the River Blyth, before crossing the dunes to return to the car parks.

Map 14

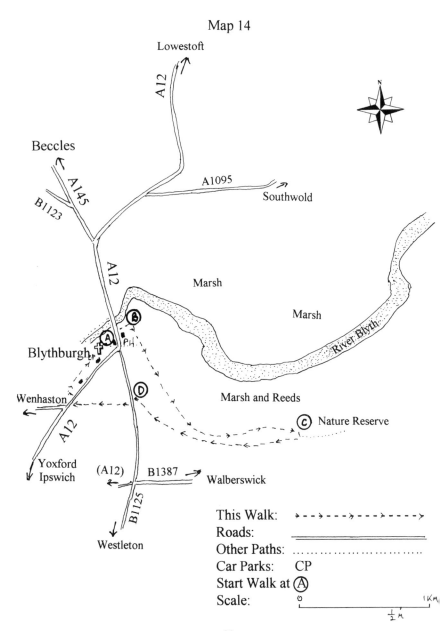

Lowestoft

A12

Beccles

A145

B1123

A12

Southwold

A1095

Marsh

Marsh

River Blyth

Blythgurgh

P.H.

Ⓐ

Ⓑ

Wenhaston

A12

Ⓓ

Marsh and Reeds

Ⓒ Nature Reserve

Yoxford
Ipswich

(A12) B1387 ➔ Walberswick

B1125

Westleton

This Walk: ➤--➤--➤--➤--➤
Roads: ───────
Other Paths: ·················
Car Parks: CP
Start Walk at Ⓐ
Scale: 0   1KM
                     ½ M

- 32 -

Walk 14

Distance: 5km (3 m) 1-1½ hours
Start Point: Blythburgh Church car park (GR 451754)
Route: The Blyth River, east of Blythburgh
Pub: White Hart, Blythburgh
Going: Easy, but **please** be careful crossing the A12.
Car Parking: Blythburgh church car park

How to get there: *Blythburgh is on the A12 about halfway between Yoxford and Wrentham. From the Yoxford direction turn left on one of the narrow side turnings to reach the church car park. (Alternatively, if you intend eating at the White Hart, it may be possible to use their car park, <u>but please ask first</u>. - this will save you two crossings of the A12 and about 1km. If starting at the pub car park, start at 'B' and finish at 'C'.*

A: Go out onto the road and follow it round past the church to the A12. Cross with great care and turn left down to the White Hart.

B: Take the unsurfaced lane from the front of the White Hart towards the river. After a few steps turn right through a gap, soon passing through a kissing gate onto the river bank. Follow this pleasant path for 2km, to reach a sign telling you to go no further unless riding a horse!

C: When you reach the sign, turn right on a signed path to reach another path in about 50m. Turn right on this track and follow it for 1½km to reach a road. *(The White Hart is about 400m along this road to the right)*

D: Cross the road to another path almost opposite. Follow this for about 500m to reach the main A12. Turn right for a short distance, then cross with great care onto the signed path opposite.

E: After a few steps go through a gap into the long field on the right. Follow the left hand edge of the field towards the church for about 150m to enter the end of a lane via a stile, and continue on towards the church. In about 200m look for a gap on the right into the church car park.

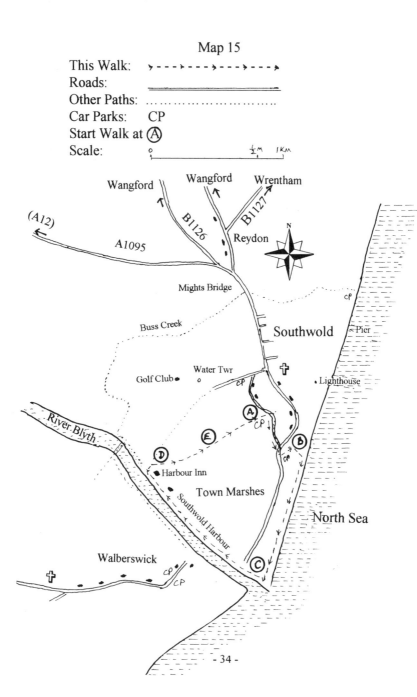

Map 15

This Walk: ›- - -›- - -›- - -›- - -›
Roads:
Other Paths: ....
Car Parks: CP
Start Walk at Ⓐ
Scale: 0   ½ᴹ   1ᴷᴹ

Wangford
Wangford   Wrentham
(A12)
B1126   B1127
A1095   Reydon
N

Mights Bridge
CP
Buss Creek   Southwold
Pier
Water Twr
Golf Club •   o   CP
✝
Lighthouse
Ⓐ
CP
River Blyth   Ⓔ
Ⓑ
Ⓓ   CP
• Harbour Inn
Town Marshes
North Sea
Southwold Harbour
Walberswick
✝   CP
CP
Ⓒ

Walk 15

Distance:	3½km (2 m) 1 hour approximately
Start Point:	Junction of Godyll Rd and Gardner Rd (GR 507761)
Route:	Southwold beach, Southwold Harbour, Town Marshes
Pub:	Harbour Inn
Going:	Easy, but see the note about the Town Marshes in '**D**'
Car Parking:	Free at the junction of Godyll Road and Gardner Road

A: Leave the car park, and turn right down Gardner Road, (signposted 'the Harbour') to reach Ferry Road in 250m. Continue along Ferry Road to pass public toilets in about 100m, then turn left on a path uphill alongside a small car park.

B: Go down onto the beach and turn right. Walk along the beach for about 1km to reach the entrance to the River Blyth.

C: Turn right along the river to reach the Harbour Inn in about 1km.

D: Immediately after passing the Harbour Inn, turn right on a narrow road, and in a few steps turn right through a gateway onto a signed path, leading diagonally across the Town Marshes. *(N.B. please note that the Town Marshes can be a bit wet after prolonged rain, or during the winter months. If you are in any doubt, you may prefer to continue up the road to pass the water tower, and onwards to reach Godyll Road where you should turn right to return to the car park)*

E: Follow the path over a series of footbridges and through the golf course to return to the car park.

Index